1,2,3, ANIMALS!

1, 2, 3, ANIMALS!

A First Counting Book for Toddlers

Bethany Lake

Illustrated by Sarah Rebar

ROCKRIDGE
PRESS

Interior and Cover Designer: Lindsey Dekker
Art Producer: Sara Feinstein
Editor: Elizabeth Baird
Production Editor: Nora Milman
Illustrations © Sarah Rebar, 2020

ISBN: Print 978-1-64611-580-8 | eBook 978-1-64739-662-6
R0

TO JOSH,

who loves and leads our crazy troupe so well.

TO CAREGIVERS AND TEACHERS

As a self-declared "math geek" and mom of four, my passion is making math fun and meaningful for kids of all ages. There are entirely too many kids who come to hate or fear math, but with the right foundation, it doesn't have to be stressful. One of the easiest ways to instill a love of numbers in your child is by reading picture books like this one together.

After simply enjoying the story together a time or two, here are some ways to dive deeper into the math on subsequent readings:

- Look for all the representations of each number. For example, on the "one" page, look for other examples of "one" to count together. There are several to choose from.

- Observe the mouse on the bottom left corners. On the first 10 left pages, they are holding up fingers that correspond to each number. This is to help your child learn the important skill of **subitizing**—that is, recognizing "how many" without counting each individual object.

- The later part of the book counts backwards from 10 as the animals put on their show. Help your child with this more advanced skill after they master counting forwards.

- Give your child additional counting prompts. You might ask, "Are there more bears or hippos?" or "Can you stomp three times like the elephants?"

- Look at the other ways to visualize the numbers 1–10 at the back of the book. These pages include additional subitizing graphics to help your child "see" quantities without counting. Find more resources at mathgeekmama.com.

My hope is that this book inspires your child to love math for many years to come.

Happy Counting!
Bethany, a.k.a. "Math Geek Mama"

The animals are on their way,
as happy as can be.
Where are they going?
How many are there?
Let's all count and see!

One lion wearing **one** top hat
is such a dapper gent.

2

Two goofy dogs with two red noses join him in the tent.

Three elephants strike **three** round drums,
their trunks raised high and proud.

Four kangaroos bring **four** snack carts
to feed a hungry crowd.

Five hippos toss their **five** batons
so high up in the air.

6

Six playful seals balance their
six bouncy balls with care.

Seven bears in **seven** tutus
leap and twirl with grace.

Eight tigers carry **eight** balloons,
in time to take their place.

9

Nine big apes spin **nine** round plates,
they know just where to go.

Ten toucans with **ten** trumpets
say it's time to start the show!

The lion stands at center stage
and gives a cheery grin.

In the tent, they're all lined up.
The show can now begin.

Ten toucans shine the spotlights.

Nine apes make quite a sight.

Eight tigers ride in circles.

Seven bears twirl in delight.

Six seals bounce their balls beside
five hippos on parade.

Four kangaroos pass around
the snacks and lemonade.

Three elephants stomp to the beat.

Two silly dogs poke fun.

And at long last, the one lone
lion says the show is done.

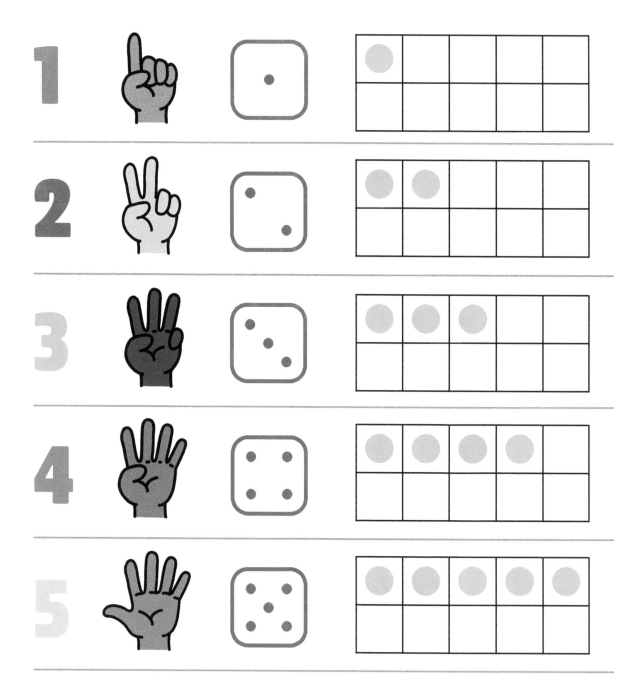

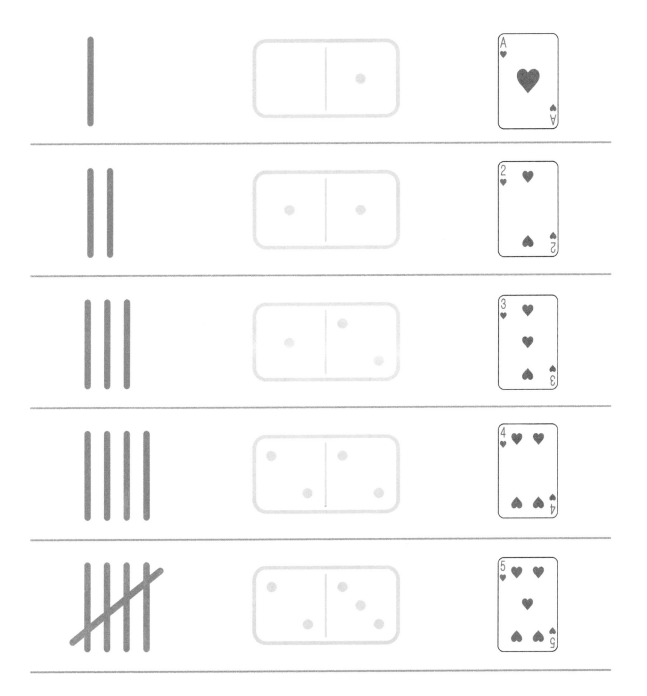

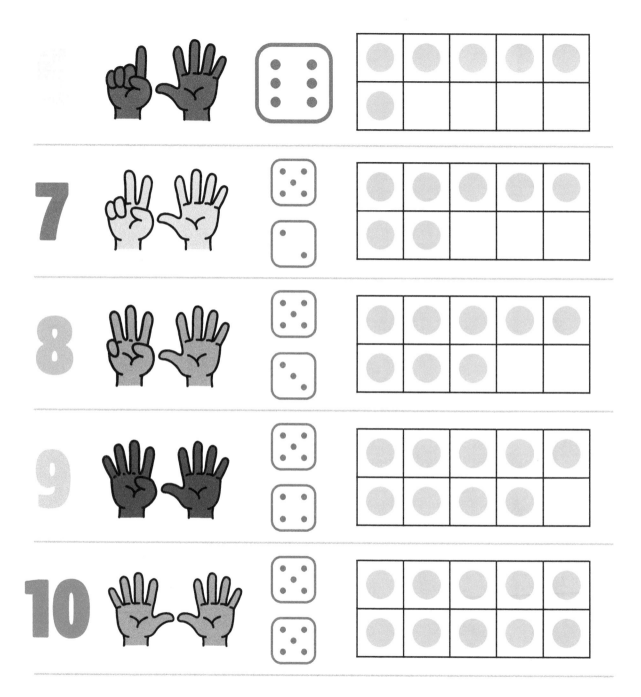

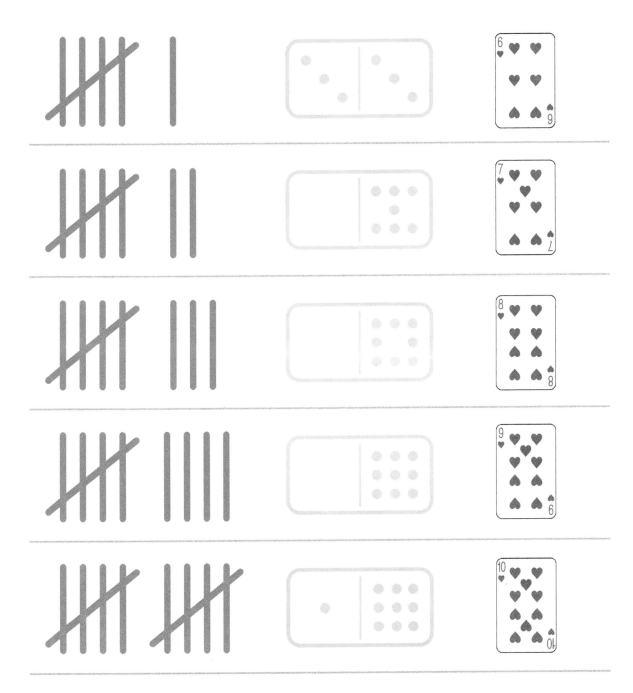

ABOUT THE AUTHOR

Bethany Lake is a former classroom teacher turned homeschool mom who specializes in math education. On her website, mathgeekmama. com, she shares easy, engaging, and meaningful ways to instill a love and excitement for math in every child. On her site, classroom teachers can find free teaching materials as well as additional ideas to explore math with picture books. She lives in Tennessee with her husband and four children.

ABOUT THE ILLUSTRATOR

Sarah Rebar is an illustrator based in sunny Los Angeles, California. She earned her BFA in illustration at Syracuse University. She worked behind-the-scenes as an artist/character designer for the kids' TV show, *Sesame Street*, for nearly 10 years in New York City! Her all-time favorite muppets are Bert and Ernie. She currently freelances for kids' TV and books in California.